WE ARE TIED
TO THE OCEAN.
AND WHEN
WE GO BACK
TO THE SEA,
WHETHER IT IS
TO SAIL OR
TO WATCH,
WE ARE GOING BACK
FROM WHENCE
WE CAME.

TIMID MEN PREFER THE CALM
OF DESPOTISM
TO THE TEMPESTUOUS SEA
OF LIBERTY.

YOU SHALL ALWAYS

CHERISH THE SEA

LET THERE BE
SPACES
IN YOUR TOGETHERNESS
AND LET THE WINDS
OF THE HEAVENS
DANCE
BETWEEN YOU.
LOVE
ONE ANOTHER
BUT MAKE NOT
A BOND
OF LOVE:
LET IT RATHER BE
A MOVING SEA
BETWEEN THE SHORES
OF YOUR SOULS.

THERE IS A TIDE
IN THE AFFAIRS
OF MEN,
WHICH TAKEN AT THE FLOOD,
LEADS ON TO FORTUNE.
OMITTED,
ALL THE VOYAGE
OF THEIR LIFE
IS BOUND
IN SHALLOWS
AND IN MISERIES.
ON SUCH A FULL SEA
ARE WE NOW AFLOAT.
AND WE MUST
TAKE THE CURRENT
WHEN IT SERVES,
OR LOSE OUR VENTURES.

MY

BONNiE

LiES

OVER

THE

OCEAN

FISHES LIVE IN THE SEA,
AS MEN DO A-LAND;
THE GREAT ONES
EAT UP
THE LITTLE ONES.

THE BOISTEROUS SEA
OF LIBERTY
IS NEVER WITHOUT
A WAVE.

AND LIFE AND DEATH
ARE ONE,
EVEN AS THE RIVER AND THE SEA
ARE ONE.

NOW   HEAR   THE
SAiLORS
    CRY,

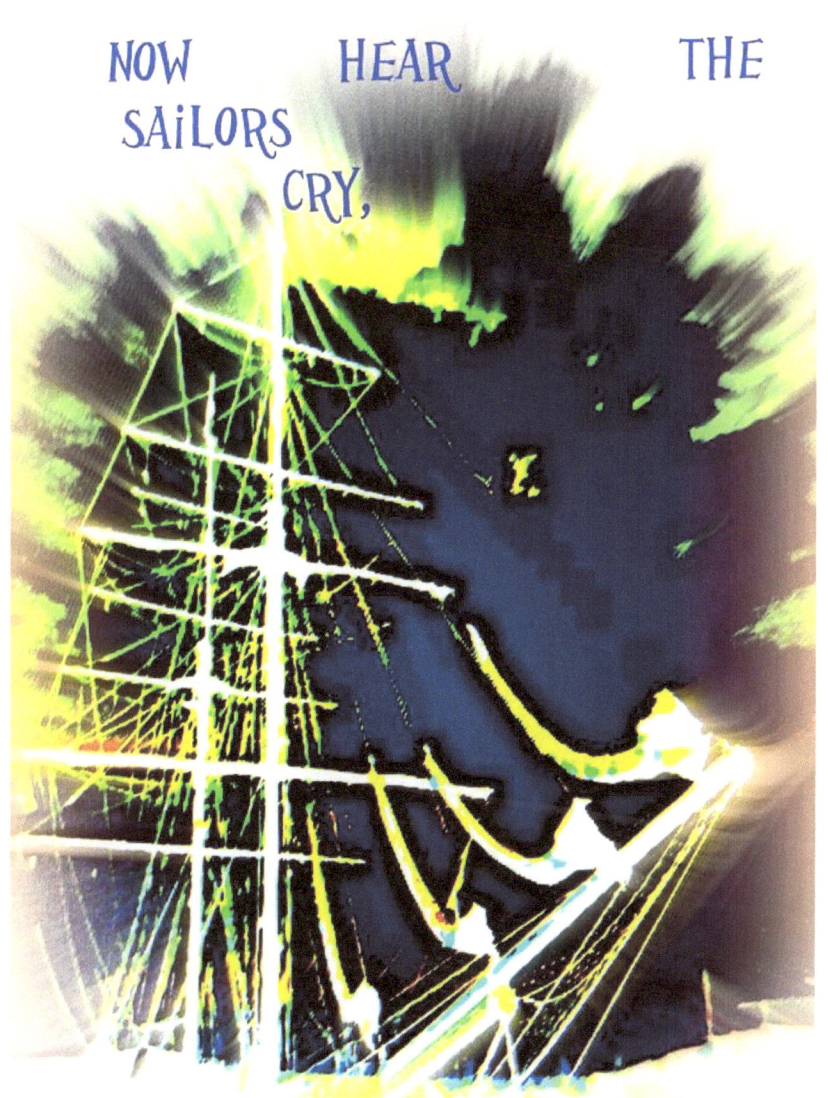

SMELL THE SEA,
        AND FEEL THE SKY

IF YOU WANT
TO BUILD A SHIP,
DON'T DRUM UP PEOPLE
TO COLLECT WOOD
AND DON'T ASSIGN THEM
TASKS AND WORK,
BUT RATHER
TEACH THEM
TO LONG
FOR THE ENDLESS
IMMENSITY
OF THE SEA.

MY SOUL iS FULL OF LONGiNG

FOR THE SECRET

OF THE SEA

MEN GO ABROAD
TO WONDER
AT THE HEIGHTS
OF MOUNTAINS,
AT THE HUGE WAVES
OF THE SEA,
AT THE LONG COURSES
OF THE RIVERS,
AT THE VAST COMPASS
OF THE OCEAN,
AT THE CIRCULAR MOTIONS
OF THE STARS,
AND THEY PASS BY
THEMSELVES
WITHOUT WONDERING.

BREAKING

WAVES

OF

CHANGE

WE MUST FREE OURSELVES
OF THE HOPE THAT
THE SEA
WILL EVER REST.
WE MUST LEARN
TO SAIL
IN HIGH WINDS.

THE WATER
OF THE SEA
RECEIVED BY THE CLOUDS
IS ALWAYS SWEET.

THE SEA

HATES

A COWARD

THE WATER
IN A VESSEL
IS SPARKLING;
THE WATER
IN THE SEA
IS DARK.

THE SMALL TRUTH
HAS WORDS
WHICH ARE CLEAR;
THE GREAT TRUTH
HAS GREAT
SILENCE.

YOU CAN'T CROSS THE SEA
MERELY BY STANDING
AND STARING
AT THE WATER.

THE FISHERMEN KNOW
THAT THE SEA
IS DANGEROUS
AND THE STORM
TERRIBLE,
BUT
THEY HAVE NEVER FOUND
THESE DANGERS
SUFFICIENT REASON
FOR REMAINING
ASHORE.

A MAN TAKETH HIS SWORD,

AND GOETH

HIS WAY

TO ROB

AND

TO STEAL,

TO SAIL

UPON THE SEA AND

UPON RIVERS

THE SEA,
ONCE IT CASTS ITS SPELL,
HOLDS YOU IN ITS NET
OF WONDER
FOREVER.

A BOOK
MUST BE THE AX
FOR THE FROZEN SEA
WITHIN US.

THE SEA DOES NOT REWARD
THOSE WHO ARE TOO ANXIOUS,
TOO GREEDY OR
TOO IMPATIENT.

THERE IS ONE SPECTACLE
GRANDER THAN THE SEA,
THAT IS THE SKY;
THERE IS ONE SPECTACLE
GRANDER THAN THE SKY,
THAT IS THE INTERIOR
OF THE SOUL.

THE VIRTUES
ARE LOST IN SELF-INTEREST
AS RIVERS
ARE LOST IN THE SEA.

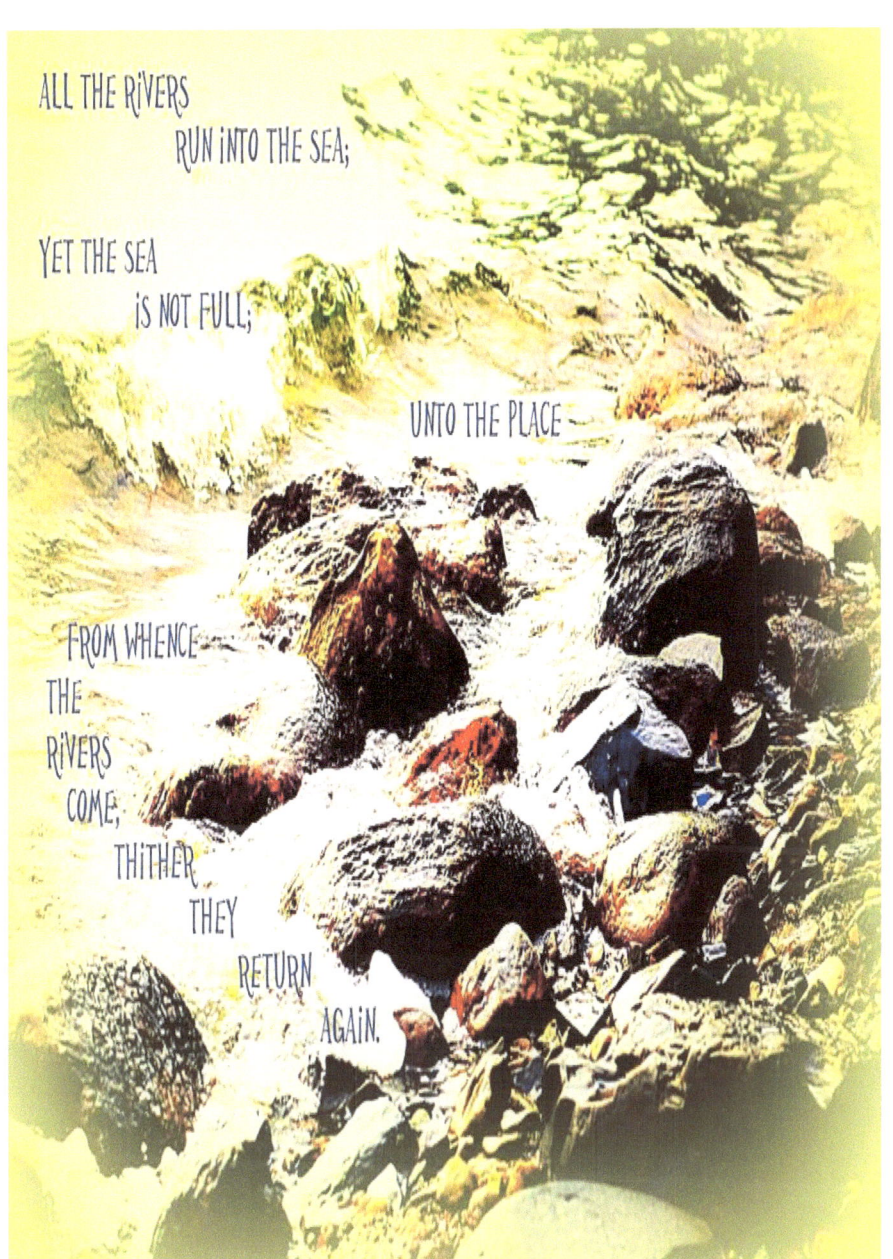

ALL THE RIVERS
RUN INTO THE SEA;

YET THE SEA
IS NOT FULL;

UNTO THE PLACE

FROM WHENCE
THE
RIVERS
COME,
THITHER
THEY
RETURN
AGAIN.

THE CURE FOR ANYTHING
IS SALT WATER:
SWEAT,
TEARS OR THE SEA.

THE MOUNTAINS,
THE FOREST,
AND THE SEA,
RENDER MEN SAVAGE;
THEY DEVELOP THE FIERCE,
BUT YET DO NOT DESTROY
THE HUMAN.

LITTLE DOVE,
BRING ME
YOUR LETTER.

PROBABLY
IT IS FROM
MY MOTHER,
BECAUSE I HAVE
WRITTEN TO HER.

LITTLE BIRD, FLY BACK AND
BRING A WINK TO MY MOTHER.
ONE DAY, WHEN I GET OLD, I WILL ACCOMPANY YOU.

AS FIRE
WHEN THROWN INTO WATER
IS COOLED DOWN
AND PUT OUT,
SO ALSO
A FALSE ACCUSATION
WHEN BROUGHT AGAINST
A MAN
OF THE PUREST AND
HOLIEST CHARACTER,
BOILS OVER
AND IS AT ONCE DISSIPATED,
AND VANISHES
AND THREATS OF HEAVEN
AND SEA,
HIMSELF STANDING
UNMOVED.

LET ME LOOK INTO A HUMAN EYE;

IT IS BETTER THAN TO GAZE

INTO SEA OR SKY

THEY ARE ILL DISCOVERERS
THAT THINK
THERE IS NO LAND,
WHEN THEY CAN SEE NOTHING
BUT SEA.

THE SEA
HAS NEITHER MEANING
NOR PITY.

THERE IS NOTHING
SO DESPERATELY
MONOTONOUS
AS THE SEA,
AND I DON'T WONDER
AT THE CRUELTY
OF PIRATES.

WE MUST PLANT THE SEA
AND HERD ITS ANIMALS
USING THE SEA AS FARMERS
INSTEAD OF HUNTERS.
THAT IS WHAT CIVILIZATION
IS ALL ABOUT
FARMING
REPLACING HUNTING.

ANYONE
CAN HOLD THE HELM
WHEN THE SEA
IS CALM.

PLEASANT IT IS,
WHEN OVER A GREAT SEA
THE WINDS TROUBLE THE WATERS,
TO GAZE FROM SHORE
UPON ANOTHER'S
GREAT TRIBULATION;
NOT BECAUSE
ANY MAN'S TROUBLES
ARE A DELECTABLE JOY,
BUT BECAUSE TO PERCEIVE
YOU ARE FREE OF THEM YOURSELF
IS PLEASANT.

WITH EVERY DROP
OF WATER
YOU DRINK,
AND WITH EVERY BREATH
YOU TAKE,
YOU ARE CONNECTED
TO THE SEA.
NO MATTER
WHERE ON EARTH
YOU LIVE.

THE SEA
IS THE UNIVERSAL
SEWER.

MY
BONNIE
LIES
OVER
THE
SEA

FROM TOO MUCH LOVE
OF LIVING,
FROM HOPE AND FEAR
SET FREE,
NO LIFE LIVES
FOR EVER;
DEAD MEN
RISE UP NEVER;
EVEN THE WEARIEST RIVER
WINDS SOMEWHERE
SAFE TO SEA.
ALL THE RIVERS RUN
INTO THE SEA;
YET THE SEA IS
NOT FULL.